Detail of the main facade (north), which was modified by Catherine de Médicis, then reinstated to its original state during the nineteenth century.

Contents

With an architecture that possesses all the elegance of the French Renaissance and a history determined by a handful of extraordinary women, the Château of Chenonceau proves to be one of the finest jewels of the Loire valley. This special issue of *Connaissance des Arts* invites you to discover an illustrious sixteenth-century residence whose distinguishing feature is its remarkable bridge-gallery crossing the Cher river.

Cover: A classic image of Chenonceau, showing how the castle is anchored in the waters of the Cher.

Left: Renovated in the nineteenth century the main facade recovered its original appearance with its monumental entrance.

4 Preface
By Alain Decaux, historian and member of the Académie Française.

6 Renaissance
Bernard Voisin, curator of Chenonceau since 1952, gives an account of the renovation work that revitalized the castle, now one of the monuments that attracts the greatest number of visitors.

14 Ladies of Chenonceau
From Katherine Bohier to Marguerite Pelouze, Axelle de Gigneron presents the seven women who determined the destiny of the estate over a period of four centuries.

28 A Treasure in Stone
Begun after 1513, the castle's construction continued throughout the sixteenth century. By Jean Guillaume, professor at the Sorbonne.

44 The Women's Gallery
Created in 2000, the Women's Gallery stages wax figures to tell the story of Chenonceau's greatest moments. Didier Moulin, art historian, takes us on a tour of this new attraction.

54 Nature Sets the Stage
Both Diane de Poitiers and Catherine de Médicis were to grace the castle with magnificent gardens that served as settings for extravagant celebrations. By Ivan Cloulas.

74 General Information

On the left side
of the building, we see
the chapel. To the right
is the Marques tower,
a vestige of the
medieval castle.

Opposite page:
The ceiling in Catherine
de Médicis's study,
which is known
as the Green Study.

Preface By Alain Decaux, historian, member of the Académie Française.

With France's innumerable patrimonial riches – landscapes, monuments, and historical sites that mark and personify the country – how can one go about choosing a favorite? It might be argued that no one asks a parent which child they prefer. As impossible as it may seem, I shall take my chances: I choose the Châteaux of the Loire.

Nature may have provided the setting, but men and women managed to use it with such artfulness that it appears as if God made the Loire, the Cher, the Indre, and the Vienne flow through Touraine just to set the stage for these castles.

Fortified castles had their day. Our favorites, the Châteaux of the Loire, required a new kind of harmony that would allow the style brought back from Italy by Charles VIII and Louis XIII to reach its full potential. Henceforth, the Loire and the Renaissance were eternally linked.

Paradoxically, beauty found its ideal setting there at a time of terrible bloodshed in France. The Loire valley became a haven of security for Francis II, Charles IX, and Henry III. Indeed, our kings loved the Loire and its tributaries because, there, they felt far away from their enemies who where always ready to attack our borders and from the frequent turmoil of the capital. Enveloped by a light that is like no other, calmed by the singular mildness of the climate, bathed in a kind of symphony that rises up from the water toward the sky, they could feel the pulse of what they called "sweet France" more strongly than anywhere else.

Little by little, the war apparatus of fortresses disappeared. Parts were preserved, simply out of reluctance to make a complete break from one's ancestral dwelling. Grace and charm replaced the heavy ramparts rendered useless by the advent of artillery. Kings were not the only ones to build: the great lords in their entourage, as well as rich businessmen and financiers set up magnificent residences near the royal estates. This was the case with Chenonceau.

There, it is as if Diane de Poitiers, the duchess of Valentinois and royal mistress, were still watching over the site. When she decided to create a garden sit for royal visits there, owners of the most beautiful estates in Touraine eagerly sent her highly-prized gifts of exotic fruit trees, and artichoke and melon plants.

On the site of a former water mill, it was Diane de Poitiers who asked Philibert de l'Orme to build a bridge across the Cher in order to link the castle to the left bank. Already a miracle, Chenonceau thus became unique.   A. D.

Just like Azay-le-Rideau, which was constructed in the same time period, Chenonceau was built on the banks of a river. This choice of site is hardly accidental, for it allows the architecture to dominate the surrounding landscape.

Renaissance

In the early 1950s, the Menier family decided to restore the entire estate.

This awesome task came under the direction of Bernard Voisin, who recounts here nearly

half a century in the service of this historical dwelling.

"In the heart of Touraine, the Garden of France, the passion of ladies and the favor of kings gave rise to the Château of Chenonceau. One after the other, five centuries of history have witnessed its birth, made it grow, embellished it, accorded it their most beautiful festivities and their most brilliant splendors, then let it drift off to sleep in the peaceful flow of the Cher.

Chenonceau has lost nothing of its mystery; motionless, it floats in the gentle light of the Loire valley. A miracle of balance in which the last Gothic blazes enhance Renaissance simplicity and the French spirit fully illuminates Italian sensuality, the castle of Diane and Catherine, the Ladies' Castle, has made its way through the ages like an enigmatic smile imbued with love and time."

This prologue to a short text, which I prepared some years ago, principally to present the castle to our visitors while paying homage to the women who lent it all their womanly virtues of beauty, charm, elegance, and grace, evokes the slumber that befell Chenonceau, overcome by a

great fatigue after centuries of glory. Indeed, by the early 1950s, with the end of the second millennium in sight, Chenonceau was peacefully dozing in the languor of its Tourainese dreams. It might well have become the "Sleeping Castle of Beauties on the Cher," but as the following decades were to show, that was nothing more than a long historical nap.

In the summer of 1951, Mr. and Mrs. Hubert Menier decided to pull the property out of its pernicious lethargy. They entrusted the direction of the vineyard to me and, then at the beginning of 1952, the responsibility of preserving the castle.

Fifty years later, I have been invited here to describe the rebirth that gave Chenonceau a new life and a new impetus that turned it into one of the most visited monuments.

Back then, the situation was hardly encouraging. Prolonged slumbering inevitably becomes harmful for a monument. It inevitably engenders damages that could only be prevented by regular maintenance. And indeed, this handsome architectural vessel anchored in the riverbed did not escape the problems that befall edifices abandoned to fate and time.

With everything waiting to be done, the question was where to begin? The castle, the Marques tower, the chancellery, the Domes which used to house the royal stables? The roofs were crying out to the roofers with all their missing pieces of slate. The outbuildings were in even worse condition than the castle itself. In the magnificent late-sixteenth-century outbuildings, which today form Chenonceau's hamlet, the excesses of time and negligence had done their damage. Here, the fine slate of Anjou, so dear to the poet Joachim du Bellay, had been replaced by the same Tourainese tiles that cover many French provincial residences.

Clearly, the most urgent task was to protect all of the buildings from further water damage: for a monument born on the piers of a mill rising up from a riverbed, this was the least that could be done. So we went to work. An agenda for putting things back in order was established and quickly carried out. The parks and gardens had also suffered greatly from so many years of slumber. While the former site of Catherine de Médicis's garden was more or less spared, the flooding of the Cher on 7 May 1940 had devastated that of Diane de Poitiers. And as one can imagine, the

In César de Vendôme's bedroom, two seventeenth-century wooden caryatids flank the west window.

Left: The balustraded crown and lateral dormer window of the west facade.

ensuing war years did not help. The park's undergrowth was cleared away; the two gardens had their wounds bandaged and soon resumed their historical role. Enclosures of lush grass lined with flowers and set among the foliage along the river, they roll out the noble perspectives of their architecture like a magic carpet at the foot of the jewel rising above them.

The vineyard, which was once so dear to Diane and Catherine, had also fallen prey to the pervading lethargy, and their vines were begging for a thorough renovation. The slopes bordering both sides of the Cher were thus replanted with choice grapes, which produce wines that have acquired a prestigious reputation over the years.

With the castle and its outbuildings protected from the rain, the gardens and parks restored in all their beauty, and the vineyard entirely replanted, all that remained was to promote this magnificent heritage from the Renaissance, in the service of both culture and tourism.

The time had come to devise methods and operations that would make the visit to the castle, its gardens, and its park ever more attractive. Innovative measures quickly presented themselves. Underlying all of them was the premise that our visitors are guests, and thus they must to be welcomed as such. The implementation of unguided visits under the discrete supervision of the security guards perfectly exemplifies this concern for an attentive and considerate welcome worthy of one's guests. The merits of such an approach no longer need to be proven; visitors confirm them every day as they gladly assume the responsibility implied by the great freedom they enjoy.

Over the past fifty years, numerous efforts have enriched this policy under the auspices of the Menier family, which bears the prestigious responsibility of preserving this important architectural heritage. Very early on, it became apparent that it would be incongruous for today's guests to suffer the slightest boredom in this residence that was once dedicated to pleasure. Thus every possible effort was made so that the brief excursion of our visitors, passengers for a day on this sumptuous vessel anchored in the bed of the Cher, would be ever more pleasant and attractive. One of the first customs at Chenonceau, which is humble and discreet but embodies the high-quality welcome that has

Reconstitution of the south facade of Thomas Bohier's castle on the Cher (drawing by Félix Roguet preserved in the castle's collection). At the center, French doors open onto a balcony.

Opposite page: The west facade with Thomas Bohier's square main building, the first two arches of the bridge built by Philibert de l'Orme for Diane de Poitiers, and a section of the gallery.

become fundamental there, is that the castle's many rooms are decorated with fresh flowers from the garden every day.

In terms of culture, there are two main points of interest: the new Women's Gallery and the annual painting and sculpture exhibition. The former royal stables housed a wax museum before they were renovated and restored in 2000 to become the Women's Gallery. Through twelve historical tableaux, this place breathes life into Chenonceau's greatest moments, from the Renaissance to the early twentieth century (see article on page 44). And then, every year, contemporary artists are given the opportunity to show their works in the prestigious setting of the Médicis Gallery, which was built on the bridge designed by Philibert de l'Orme. The success of these exhibitions celebrates Chenonceau's marriage of culture and tourism. Artists such as Brasilier, Fassianos, Bardone, Cathelin, Génis, Weisbuch, Boncompain, the Lalannes, and Mytaras have delighted millions of viewers.

Chenonceau has come down to us over the course of more than four centuries, during which it often played an important role in French history. Moored on its anchors of stone, this castle seems to defy the passage of time. Bathed in Touraine's gentle light, it stands erect in all the splendor of its beauty – a luminous jewel radiant like a woman's smile. B. V.

Above: the ceiling in Thomas Bohier's study bears his initials (TB) along with that of his wife Katherine (TK). This is the oldest surviving example of an Italian-style coffered ceiling in France.

Right: Lit by three windows overlooking the Cher, Thomas Bohier's office possesses all the characteristics of a "private study."

Catherine de Médicis built upon Diane de Poitiers and Philibert de l'Orme's plans to construct a gallery on the Cher. Stretching over sixty meters, it consists of two galleries, one on top of the other.

Ladies of Chenonceau

Throughout its long history, Chenonceau had been built and run by women.

Axelle de Gaigneron describes the personalities of these seven exceptional ladies who made

the estate one of the treasures of the Loire valley.

Ladies of the court, ladies of the heart, women with savvy and a sense of business: seven women, two of them queens, determined the fate of Chenonceau. This feminine control over a castle and its estate is not only exceptional for its scope and continuity – we could say it was Chenonceau's destiny – but also for the strong personalities of the successive owners and their roles in history. In isolated cases, however, this situation arose more often than one would think, notably with the absence of husbands called away to war or other affairs of the kingdom. Take for example, the Château of Azay-le-Rideau, which is in the same region and which was rebuilt by a woman, the beautiful Philippe [sic] Lesbahy, also during the Renaissance. In any case, Chenonceau admirably demonstrates that "life in a castle" was not what the expression implies, and far from being an exercise in frivolity, it often represented a strong, solid task. By exercising their authority in matters of taste and their managerial skill in agriculture, forestry, viticulture, horticulture, and administration, the ladies of Chenonceau left behind a heritage of

Right: The young window of Louis de Brezé, Diane de Poitiers (1499–1566), became the mistress of Henry II who was nineteen years her junior. She exerted considerable influence on him in both political matters and artistic taste.

Left: Diane de Poitiers's former bedroom. The fireplace is attributed to Jean Goujon, a French sculptor of the Ecole de Fontainebleau. The portrait of her rival, Catherine de Médicis, is a modern work.

Diane de Poitiers, 2ᵉ femme de Louis de Brezé Grand Seneschal de Normandie, créée Duchesse de Valentinois par Henri II en 1548.

LA·GRANT·SENECHALLE

architecture, ornament, and landscape gardening (notwithstanding the successive reorganizations that have had their own logic) that is among the first and most striking in France. Let us have a look, then, at these seven women who ran Chenonceau.

Katherine Bohier (?–1526)

With her, Chenonceau entered court life by a powerful channel. Wife of Thomas Bohier, finance minister of Normandy, Katherine Bohier was the daughter of Guillaume Briçonnet and niece of Jacques de Semblançay, both finance superintendents. This was the sphere of the kingdom's great financiers, all of whom were related by blood or interests in Touraine.

Under Katherine's direction, both the building, begun after 1513, and the estate came under real management for the first time. She took over the reins and held onto them, by character, education, and resources. "These financial circles," wrote the historian Jean-Pierre Babelon, "consisted of people with taste and money, people with audacity as well, who unhesitatingly flaunted their wealth. There was a long tradition of this. There was Jacques Cœur in Bourges, Fouquet in Vaux-le-Vicomte . . . French architecture owes much to these people." The construction program and the administration

of Chenonceau were no small affair, given the scale of the site itself and what it represented to society. The chapel, for example, was consecrated by Cardinal Bohier, a relative. Francis I paid two visits. Receiving the king was no minor affair; it required perfect knowledge of the customs of the royal court.

Thomas Bohier died in 1524, and Katherine, two years later. She left behind a ship that had been well launched. Chenonceau was passed onto her son Antoine Bohier. However, an official audit ordered by the king (who also sentenced Uncle Semblançay to the gallows) fined Antoine a colossal sum. When a settlement was reached, Chenonceau belonged to Francis I who had always been fascinated by it. Thus, Chenonceau, property of the Crown, became the royal residence. This was the doing of a debt; a love affair was to get Chenonceau out of it.

Diane de Poitiers (1499–1566)

Wife of Louis de Brézé, grand seneschal of France, and lady-in-waiting to the queen, Diane de Poitiers possessed both beauty, which was captured in famous portraits such as *Diana the Huntress* at the Louvre, and an extremely acute intelligence and sense of business. The latter was well served by

The sixteenth-century Flemish tapestry *Triomphe de la force* finds its place in Diane de Poitiers's bedroom.

Following page: François Clouet (circa 1510–1572), *Le Bain de Diane*, oil on wood, 136 x 96.5 cm, Musée des Beaux-Arts, Rouen. This painting celebrates the triumph of Mary Stuart, the "new Diane" who had just married Catherine de Médicis's son Francis II. Her features can be recognized in the seated nymph.

the passion she aroused in the dauphin, the future Henry II. It is well known that he lavished her with honors – she became duchess of Valentinois – as well as with fabulous jewels and other gifts. It was Diane who built the Château of Anet, one of France's architectural treasures and, in 1547, Henry II gave her Chenonceau, under the guise of a courtly pretext: a gift commemorating the "great and commendable services" rendered to the Crown by her late husband. Diane, however, intended to consolidate her property.

A superb feat of legal magic soon followed. She managed to have Antoine Bohier's settlement canceled, which removed Chenonceau from Crown control all the while making Bohier her debtor and thus cornering him into a sale. In a final ploy, Chenonceau was put up for auction and awarded to Diane over other bidders.

Her subsequent operational strategy was exemplary. The first step consisted of inventorying the premises and their contents, which turned out to be insufficient to finance the anticipated changes and additions. The second step therefore was to make Chenonceau profitable. Surrounding herself with experienced administrative counselors, many of whom were royal officers, she took charge of everything. And "everything" meant supervising the income from her rights as owner of the castle (tithes, notary deeds, leases, etc), including the forest, the livestock rearing, the land under cultivation, the vineyards, and the sale of produce at the market. Her light red wine production prospered, as did her yellow peach orchards, to which the duchess added a patch of mulberry trees for the cultivation of silkworms.

The third step was making Chenonceau the model of perfection that would satisfy her craving for glory. Along with architectural renovations, Diane de Poitiers endowed Chenonceau with some of the most spectacular and modern gardens of the time, where a multitude of species decorated a subtle geometry of beds and paths punctuated with fountains. A kitchen garden with an equally splendid layout included innumerable fruits, vegetables, and flowers, both common and rare. No destiny outlasts time, however, and just as her fleeting celebrations were to vanish, Diane de Poitiers was obliged to cede Chenonceau to

Upstairs, the Bedchamer of the Five Queens evokes the memory of Catherine de Médicis's two daughters and three daughters-in-law: Elisabeth de France, Margaret of Valois, Marie Stuart, Elizabeth of Austria, and Louise of Lorraine.

Left: Catherine de Médicis's bedchamber is decorated with a group of sixteenth-century Flemish tapestries recounting the life of Samson.

Right: Catherine de Médicis (1519–1589), drawing by François Clouet, Bibliothèque Nationale de France, Paris. Daughter of Lorenzo de Médicis II, the duke of Urbino, Catherine de Médicis played a major role in the management of state affairs when she became regent upon the accession of her son Charles IX.

Catherine de Médicis upon the death of Henry II. The estate reverted to the Crown.

Catherine de Médicis (1519–1589)

Widow of Henry II, and mother of Francis II, Charles IX (during whose minority she served as regent), and Henry III. Ambitious, authoritarian, and endowed with a diabolical intelligence befitting her Florentine origins, she brought Chenonceau and the life that was led there to new heights of splendor, celebration, and profit, and all this in the midst of the Wars of Religion. Aside from pursuing architectural and decorative renovations, she also further developed the operation set up by her predecessor and rival Diane de Poitiers by importing vines from Champagne and transforming an already excellent vineyard into one of the best. Similarly, she increased the silkworm cultivation, had the silk spun on the estate, and created the "queen's cloth," which was woven in Orléans. She also significantly increased the estate's income, once again, by reappraising the tenant farms, smallholdings, mills, woods, and rights of castellany. Lastly, she extended the gardens even more lavishly, particularly with the introduction of lemon and orange trees. Drawing on her Italian flair for gardening, she created a splendidly balanced space with beds, multiple groves, grottos, pergolas, and fountains – including the Fountain of the Rock, which is adorned with animals sculpted by Bernard Palissy. And finally, she masterminded the art of celebrations and elevated them to their theatrical heights. There was no lack of merrymaking at Chenonceau, nor was there a shortage

Louise of Lorraine, anonymous sixteenth-century drawing, Bibliothèque Nationale de France, Paris. The hapless wife of a king who preferred the company of his male acolytes. After the assassination of Henry III in 1589, Queen Louise spent the last eleven years of her life surrounded by nuns and dressed in white, the color of royal mourning. She had the black walls of her bedroom painted with the emblems of death (as reconstituted here).

of licentiousness. Two celebrations in particular have gone down in history.

The first was organized in 1560 in honor of Francis II and his wife, Mary Stuart. Directed by Primaticcio with the participation of Ronsard, Baïf, Dorat, and Jodelle, this festive spectacle, set against a backdrop of triumphal arches, baths, and ancient Tuscan-style colonnades welcomed the youthful couple with the thunder of canons, fireworks, and nine hundred drums.

In 1577, the second festivity brought together three queens – Catherine, Louise (wife of Henry III), and Margaret of Navarre (wife of the future Henry IV). The splendor of the event was coupled with extraordinary ambiguity: beneath the brocades, pearls, and precious stones, half of the women were semi-nude, and the other half, dressed as men; following the lead of Henry III and his effeminate favorites, men dressed as women. The confusion was such that: "At first sight everyone had difficulty [knowing] if he was looking at a female king or a male queen." All of this was accompanied by violins and Commedia dell'arte performers from Italy. But as always, the current of time continued to flow. Following the death of Catherine de Médicis, Chenonceau's laughter gave way to tears.

Queen Louise (1553–1601)

Wife of Henry III, Louise of Lorraine-Vaudémont inherited Chenonceau from Catherine de Médicis. She was just as eager to take charge, but with a heavy heart: not only was she enamored with a man who loved only men, but she never got over his death. After the king's assassination in 1589, she transformed Chenonceau into a tomb. Nonetheless, this tomb was perfectly maintained and controlled, estate and castle alike. Within the castle draped in black, the queen roamed about dressed in white, the color of royal mourning. She surrounded herself with nuns who frequented the estate as if it were a convent and her acts of charity earned her the nickname "the White Lady of Chenonceau." Together with the sad queen, the splendors of this Loire castle and the house of Valois passed on; after her death, Chenonceau was to sink into a destructive slumber of neglect.

The Duchess of Vendôme (1592–1669)

Daughter of Philippe Emmanuel de Mercœur-Vaudémont and wife of César de Vendôme, the illegitimate son of Henry IV and Gabrielle d'Estrées, Françoise de Mercœur, duchess of Vendôme, set out to oversee Chenonceau with

Portrait of Louise Dupin by Jean-Marc Nattier (1685–1766), o/c, 63.5 x 74.5 cm. The daughter of a member of the Comédie Française, Louise Dupin held a philosophical and literary salon at Chenonceau. In the Age of Enlightenment, the castle was frequented by figures such as Voltaire, Rousseau, and Montesquieu.

the same order and rigor as all of its previous owners. The Bourbons, however, had little interest in the estate, except for hunting. In 1650, Louis XIV was the last ruler of the Ancien Régime to visit Chenonceau. Laid to rest by Queen Louise, Chenonceau was to be revived by the daughter of an actress in the Comédie Française.

Louise Dupin (1706–1799)

The natural daughter of the well-known financier Samuel Bernard and Manon Dancourt (later Fontaine) who came from a family of actors belonging to the Comédie Française and who became a member herself in 1684, Louise married the farmer general Claude Dupin. She was an intelligent, beautiful, and highly cultivated woman who had theater in her blood. (Claude Dupin, a widower, had a son, Louis-Claude, from his first wife, Marie Aurore of Saxony, the grandmother of George Sand. The resulting confusions, between father and son on the one hand, and between Marie Aurore and Louise Dupin on the other, have been kindly cleared up for us by the George Sand scholar Georges Lubin). The literary salon that Louise Dupin held at Chenonceau included Montesquieu, Voltaire, Buffon, Fontenelle, Marivaux, Condillac, Claudine-Alexandrine Guérin de Tencin, and the marquise of Deffand. Rousseau, who served as Dupin's secretary and tutor to her son, worked on *Emile* at Chenonceau, and as he recalled in *Confessions:* "We enjoyed ourselves a great deal there and ate very well; I became as fat as a monk. We played music and staged comedies. I wrote a play in verse entitled *Sylvie's Path,* after the name of a path in the park on the Cher." Louise Dupin died at the age of ninety-three, leaving behind the memory of the Enlightenment through her remarkable philosophical and literary salon at Chenonceau. It was due to her popularity that the estate was spared during the French Revolution. With her death, the castle fell back into a state of lethargy.

Marguerite Pelouze

Sister of Jules Grévy's future son-in-law, Marguerite took possession of Chenonceau in 1864. Caught up in the contemporary craze for revivals, she set out to restore the castle to its sixteenth-century

The bedchamber of César de Vendôme, the illegitimate son of King Henry IV and his mistress Gabrielle d'Estrées, whose bedchamber appears below. César de Vendôme became owner of Chenonceau in 1664, through his wife, Françoise de Lorraine-Mercœur, but he always preferred the Château of Anet.

appearance, a project which necessitated major renovation. She also transferred the four caryatids of Athena, Apollo, Hercules, and Cybele, from the castle to the park. Eventually, she ran out of money and Chenonceau was seized for debts in 1888. It was acquired in 1913 by the industrialist Henri Menier, founder of the chocolate factory that bears his name, and the estate has remained in the family ever since.

In lofty places such as this, memories are eventually clothed with fiction: thus, it was at Chenonceau that Eugène Scribe situated the libretto for *The Huguenots,* which was set to music by Meyerbeer. Who can resist imagining the spirited Catherine de Médicis ruling Chenonceau, which was simultaneously within and far removed from the turbulent events raging about one of the most fascinating castles in France? A. G.

A Treasure in Stone

One of the most famous architectural jewels of the Loire valley, Chenonceau

is a striking combination of local French tradition and borrowings from Italy. Jean Guillaume

traces the construction of this castle throughout the course of the sixteenth century.

Chenonceau was initially the work of Thomas Bohier, one of the leading figures of the French business elite. Completely devoted to the king, Bohier supervised his finances, lent him money, and carried out secret missions for him – and got fabulously rich in the process. Tied to the financiers of Tours, he married Katherine Briçonnet, who belonged to the same milieu and undoubtedly supervised the building activity during her husband's frequent absences. After being ennobled by the king, it became necessary for him to acquire a domain in order to maintain his rank. As early as 1496, he had purchased Chenonceau from the debt-ridden Pierre Marques, whose family had held the property since the thirteenth century, but it was only in February 1513, after seventeen years of proceedings, that Bohier finally became its owner. A year later, Louis XII confirmed this social advance by formally making Chenonceau a castellany.

Begun after 1513, its construction was undoubtedly quite advanced by December 1517, when Francis I's decree authorizing the building of a

Drawing of Chenonceau (preserved in the castle's collection) made after the construction of the bridge in 1559 and before the addition of the galleries in 1576. The little entrance to the left is furnished with a drawbridge providing access to the left bank of the Cher.

bridge over the Cher made mention of the "beautiful site and house situated on the Cher river . . . where we might occasionally stay." The castle must have been completed shortly afterward, as the chapel's gallery bears the date 1521 and roof partitions were in place by January 1522.

Bohier died in Italy in 1524, before Francis I took legal action against the financiers of Tours. It was thus his son who faced an enormous fine, which he paid off by ceding the estate to the king in 1535. Shortly after Henry II inherited the throne in 1547, he gave Chenonceau to his mistress, Diane de Poitiers. She found the castle too small, however, and in 1556 she asked Philibert de l'Orme to extend it with a gallery set on a bridge over the Cher. There was enough time for her to build the bridge, but after the death of Henry II, his widow, Catherine de Médicis, forced Diane to exchange Chenonceau for the Château of Chaumont. Fifteen years later, the queen mother herself decided to enlarge Chenonceau, and in 1576, she began construction of the massive galleries that stand on the bridge today.

After the passage of many vicissitudes in between, Chenonceau was acquired in 1864 by Marguerite Pelouze, who entrusted its restoration to Félix Roguet. She had the entrance facade, which had been modified by Catherine de Médicis, returned to its original state, built a second staircase, installed "Renaissance" fireplaces throughout, and graced the chapel with a door so finely sculpted that it could be taken for an original.

Thomas Bohier's Castle

The Marques family castle stood beside the Cher, on the moat-surrounded terrace preceding the current castle. Bohier kept nothing of the earlier building but one tower, to which he added new windows and a slightly protruding crown set on little bases that give the illusion of fortifications.

The tower served as a reminder of the previous castle and thus demonstrated the age and noble character of the site.

The new castle was built directly over the Cher on the piers of what was formerly the estate's water mill. With the exception of their cutwaters, these piers were joined by a barrel vault to form a rectangular platform. The main structure of the building has a square plan, turrets at its four corners, and an H-shaped roof – combined, these elements create an interesting play of volumes. Upstream, to the east, a chapel and a small pavilion extending to the far end of the cutwaters frame the terrace that fills the remaining portion of the rectangular platform.

Inside, a central gallery covered with handsome triangular rib vaults runs the length of the building. At each end, small stairways lead down to the kitchen and service rooms, which are housed within the piers; near the center of the gallery, a straight stairway leads to the second floor. Large double doors open onto the first room on the left,

The Marques tower (opposite) is the only vestige Thomas Bohier kept of the medieval castle. Its windows, door, and pseudo-fortifications around the crown, however, have been modified with a Renaissance style. Similar to those decorating the castle's large dormer windows, the pediment above the door (above) recalls the Francis I wing of the Château of Blois.

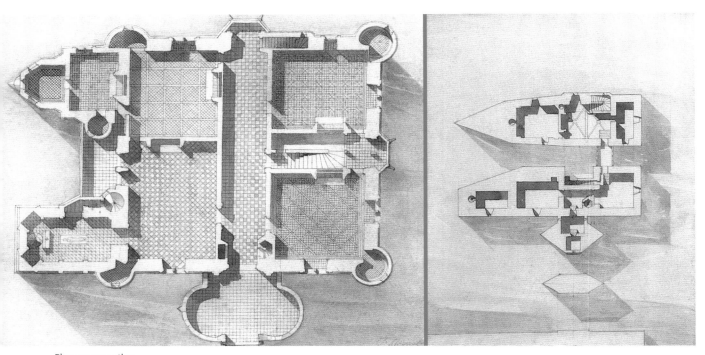

Plans representing
Thomas Bohier's castle
(drawings by Félix
Roguet preserved
in the castle's collection).
To the left are basement
rooms installed within
the hollow piers;
to the right, the ground
floor. Thomas Bohier's
apartment occupied
three southeast rooms,
the smallest one being
his "study."

Right: Constructed
on a rectangular platform,
the main building has
a nearly square plan,
which is divided
in two equal parts by
the central gallery.

where some of the original panels decorated with images of the founders' patron saints are still intact, along with Bohier's cryptic motto: "S'il vient à point me souviendra" (which has been taken to mean "If the building is finished, it will preserve my memory"). This room adjoins the chapel and the southeast bedroom, which, in turn, leads to two small rooms located in the pavilion outside. The second of these rooms has an Italian-style coffered ceiling decorated with the monograms of Bohier and his wife and it appears to be the private "study" reserved for the master of the castle. Thus Bohier probably occupied the southeast portion of the ground floor, and it would seem that Katherine Briçonnet resided above him on the same side. The other rooms, to the west, were bedrooms reached by a passageway behind the staircase.

First seen at Bury around 1512, the regular organization of plans and facades reappears at Chenonceau. The nearly square plan of the main structure was evidently a deliberate choice since the platform below is rectangular. In addition, the square is divided into two equal parts by the central gallery, which is exactly half as wide as the neighboring rooms (this modular system is also found at Chambord). In the north and west facades, the openings are distributed symmetrically and the central axis is clearly marked with wider windows,

a balcony, and a larger dormer. While the other facades are less clearly defined, there is no lack of concern for regularity. The southern facade, now half hidden by Catherine de Médicis's galleries, had a central projecting structure with cut corners (the right half of which can still be seen on the second floor), large windows, and a ground-floor balcony similar to that of the west facade. To the left, however, there was a shallow projection that enclosed the service staircase leading down to the butlery, which was too wide for the thickness of the wall. This staircase made it impossible to have a window on the left to match the one on the right, and it was necessary to settle for a half-casement. On the east side, the chapel and the pavilion were carefully given distinctive treatment: the windows do not have the same form; the moldings between stories are not at the same level, and the frieze of balusters at the top of the wall does not continue around the chapel and the pavilion (while it does run between them, above the terrace). The chapel and the pavilion are thus seen as separate buildings; together with the terrace that joins them, they make for a lively composition alongside the "uniform" castle. Finally, like at Bury, the desire for symmetry extends to the surroundings of the building – not the garden, which we know nothing about, but the avenue

Opposite page:
The castle's east facade,
where the chapel
and pavilion were carefully
designed to stand out.

One must go through
the Guardroom to get to
the chapel (below).
While the chapel's royal
gallery bears the date
1521, the current stained
glass windows were
made by the master-
glassmaker Max Ingrand.
The original ones were
damaged by bombing
in 1944. In the loggia,
there is a Virgin and
Child in Carrara marble,
dating from the sixteenth
century (left).

lined with "tall elms, holm oaks, and other beautiful trees" that leads to the castle. Its alignment with the central gallery was an exceptional arrangement for that time.

The Italian-style straight staircase was probably the second to be introduced in the Loire Valley, after that of Bury. This version is not entirely authentic, however, since the flight winds around the end of the supporting wall instead of being broken up by a landing between stories. As a result, the staircase is shorter than it would have been if it had a landing and this allowed for the addition of a passageway connecting the two neighboring rooms – the winding section bordered with a balustrade overhangs this passageway. What was the reasoning behind this arrangement? There was enough depth to accommodate a landing and a passageway underneath, so we know that it was not imperative. Conversely, the solution adopted had significant aesthetic consequences. When climbing these stairs, one sees the large

A central gallery (or vestibule) covered by ogival vaults (above) runs the length of the building. Perpendicular to this gallery, a balustrade stairway leads to a small gallery bathed in light (opposite page) on the second floor.

window behind the balustrade and the two large arcades opening onto the passageway. So clearly defined on the right-hand side, the interior space, which is framed by walls and barrel-vaulted, is no longer delimited on the window side – it gives way to the transparency characteristic of the "flamboyant" spirit. All the charm of the staircase at Chenonceau lies in this surprising contrast. Moreover, due to the passageway, there is no need for a window between stories, which always accompanies the landing of a straight staircase. The existing window – which is in fact a French window opening onto the balcony – is thus placed at the regular height; it is simply taller and wider than the others in order to provide more light for the staircase and to mark the facade's center.

Chenonceau's general arrangement, however, remains the most singular aspect of the building. Instead of the expected castle with a courtyard, along the lines of Bury or Azay, one finds a massive structure built up from out of the water.

Of course the desire to orchestrate views of the river was already manifest at Ambroise, where the great hall opens onto a balcony over the Loire, or at Gaillon, where the terrace overlooks the Seine, but the concern for linking the building to the landscape goes much further at Chenonceau. The most unusual plan of the interior gallery and the staircase off the side was born out of the site itself. Indeed, the gallery was not made to lead to the bridge planned in 1517, since this was to have been situated one kilometer upstream. Nor was it inspired by Martainville in Normandy, a castle with a massive plan similar to that of Chenonceau, since the gallery there leads to a staircase behind. In contrast, the role of the gallery in Thomas Bohier's castle is to lead to the French window overlooking the Cher. At the time, the castle's interior was not dark and closed in as it is today, but a luminous, open space. Through the window at the end of the gallery it was possible to see the opposite bank of the Cher; as one

Impost and capital
in the central gallery.
The size of the corner
motif, the sharp contrast
of the basket and abacus,
and the quality of
the sculptural ornament
are characteristic of
the period around 1515.

Right: The south facade
of Thomas Bohier's
castle is now cut through
the center by Catherine
de Médicis's galleries.
The small annex at the
corner completely hides
the old French window
on the ground floor.

approached, the river itself gradually became visible, and one more step led onto the balcony, and the full panorama of water and trees. This desire to bring the landscape into the building also explains the unusual position of the staircase. If it were not off to the side, it would have to be placed in the second half of the gallery, which would have ruined the effect of transparency. Thus it was placed perpendicular to the hall and separated by a door still in place today – a curious detail but one we now understand better. When closed, this door focuses all attention on the French window and the vista of the Cher; when open, the view through the arcades of the winding portion of the staircase yields the surprise of another luminous and open space from which, a few steps further, the whole expanse of the river can be discovered.

The precise date of such an innovation can only be determined through careful examination of decorative elements, which can then be compared with those of other castles. The pilasters adorned with three large flutes and capitals with shallow abaci recall Hôtel Barguin (Gouin) in Tours, which dates from around 1510, more than Blois and Azay. The molding of the window splays, which is rounded at the corners and lacks a wide band, is not the same as that of the castles that implemented new innovations. The right-angle string courses between stories, which permitted the introduction of large ornamental tablets, shows that the builders did not understand or simply rejected the intersection pilasters and double string courses used at Bury and Blois. The crown of the facade, which is set on gothic-like leaf-ornamented bases, has a frieze of balusters similar to that of the Grand'Maison at Gaillon, and a cornice with consoles and rosettes recalling that of the Longueville wing at Châteaudun, begun around 1510. Other features, by contrast, seem considerably more "developed": the great central dormers topped with miniature facades recall Blois and Bonnivet; the capitals and bases of the central gallery have thick abaci and an impressive sculptural decoration; the "antique" ornamentation of the keystones in the stairway, the ornamentation of the pilasters in the winding part, the foliage frieze on the door of the Marques tower, which is similar to that of Blois, are all of high quality. Indeed, above the south dormer, where it is practically invisible, there is an exceptional work of art: a frieze of nude fauns and

Above, opposite page, and next double page: Catherine de Médicis's main galleries constructed on the bridge built by Philibert de l'Orme. Sixty meters long and six meters wide, this magnificent ballroom begins at the castle's south facade and is adorned with a monumental mantlepiece at each extremity, one of them being a purely decorative frame for the south door, which opens onto a drawbridge leading to the left bank of the Cher.

hybrid creatures swept up in a furious movement, which calls to mind Zoan Andrea's engravings. Therefore, it would seem that the castle's realization was entrusted to a workshop that was indifferent to the innovations of Bury, and the influence of Blois did not make itself felt until the final stages of the project. At that point, a highly talented sculptor (or group of sculptors), familiar with the most "modern" forms of decoration, must have worked on the gallery and staircase, the large south dormer, and the Marques tower's door. While Chenonceau is perfectly harmonious in its plan, it is less coherent in its construction, which juxtaposes elements from the early Renaissance style with those of around 1515. These observations confirm what is suggested by the history of the estate and Bohier's impatience: the construction of the new castle must have begun around 1513.

The Bridge-Gallery

Diane de Poitiers found Chenonceau as Bohier had left it. In 1515, she created a vast square garden along the Cher, to the east of the castle. This garden, which has been replanted in a

different form today, is surrounded on all four sides by a dirt levee, from which visitors can admire its design, and isolated by a canal that flows into the moats of the forecourt. In Diane's time, pathways divided the garden into compartments filled with flowerbeds and fruit trees and a stream of water six meters high rose in the center. One thing the castle lacked was a grand reception hall. In 1555, Diane decided to construct a gallery for this purpose and called upon Philibert de l'Orme. Sensitive to the spirit of the site, she and the architect chose to closely link the gallery to its surroundings. Thus, the new room was to be built on a bridge over the Cher, but it would not occupy the entire width of the bridge so that guests could exit the gallery on either side and admire the river outdoors. Nor was it to extend all the way to the other bank: at its far end, there was to be a great window and a balcony "like a terrace where one could get some fresh air." Moreover, the new construction was not to alter the existing structure. Instead of being placed on the axis of the corridor, as might be expected, the bridge was shifted to the west, so that the gallery could fit between the west window and the central French window. Thus, no window was to be obstructed, and the interior gallery would still overlook the Cher. To reach the new gallery, it was necessary to open the glass door and cross the balcony. From the outside, this gallery would look like a simple annex; with its low volume enlivened by a continuous row of windows, it would have easily fitted in with the existing building. Catherine de Médicis took a totally different approach. After creating a garden on the left bank of the Cher, she decided in 1576 to transform the site entirely by constructing an enormous complex of buildings around Bohier's castle. However, the queen only managed to complete part of this project. She made a few modifications to the castle in order to gain two extra rooms on the east terrace, and on Philibert de l'Orme's bridge, she began building a group of galleries that were supposed to form an oval plan. Evidence of this can still be seen in the stonework at the galleries' furthest extremity. Filling the entire width of the bridge and rising over two stories, the new building overwhelms the Bohier castle with its mass. In addition, it partially blocks the window openings of the central bays, the right part of which (seen from the inside) was now taken up with doors leading to the new galleries. On the ground floor,

the left half was completely blocked by a small annex. This project is said to have been carried out by "the queen's architect," Jean Bullant. We, however, are not convinced, for the high relief ornamentation on the second floor is too far removed from the ornate and minutely detailed style found at Ecouen and Fère-en-Tardenois. This decoration, based on the overlapping of two motifs – segmented pediments much wider than the windows and ornamental frames that appear to support the pediments – is quite interesting. It was derived from a decorative motif created forty years earlier by Perino del Vaga on the walls of the Sala Reggia in the Vatican and it constitutes a fine example of French mannerism. This success, however, does not obscure the incongruity of the building. The singular effect of transparency sought by Thomas Bohier and respected by Diane de Poitier was to be irreparably destroyed by the galleries of Catherine de Médicis.   J. G.

The Dome building
still bears witness
to the grand unfinished
projects of the
Renaissance. Converted
into outbuildings,
then into stables during
the nineteenth century,
today, they house
the historical tour, the
Women's Gallery.

The Women's Gallery

Francis I visiting Chenonceau, Henry II having a tête-à-tête with Diane de Poitiers,

Catherine de Médicis's extravagant ball . . . Stroll through twelve scenes that revive the history

of the estate. Didier Moulin guides us through the Women's Gallery, which replaces

the castle's old wax museum.

Katherine Bohier, Diane de Poitiers, Catherine de Médicis, Louise of Lorraine, Louise Dupin . . . So many queens, women of strong will, style, and character who were to fashion one of the most beautiful estates in Val-de-Loire. Today, Chenonceau pays due homage to them by means of the Women's Gallery, which opened in the year 2000. It began with a desire to return some of Chenonceau's architectural elements to the limelight, while rekindling the memory of the great individuals who inhabited it.

Set up in the castle's outbuildings, also known as the Domes, where traces of Jacques Androuet du Cerceau's Grand Project for Catherine de Médicis are still visible, the Women's Gallery allows these buildings, which were until then largely ignored, to regain the public's attention. For these outbuildings, which were later converted into stables and thoroughly modified throughout the course of centuries, still possess a Renaissance volume and contain some original historical elements in the current masonry work.

The layout of the former stables can be discerned

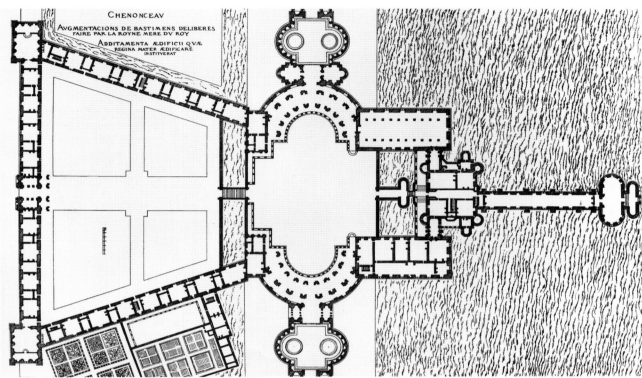

through a plan delineated by bricks in the ground
It was also necessary to uncover the dividing walls
to make visible the initial interior arrangement.
The project is based on these exposed historical
spaces, using the old traces as a regulating line
for the development of contemporary facilities.
Moreover, the facade has regained a presence
that the previous restorations had erased, particularly through the addition of two awnings that are
adaptations of royal canopies and benches
based on the design of historical models of
garden furniture.

A Genuine Historical Interpretation

Working on historical content implies guaranteeing
its quality for visitors, no matter what museologi-
cal techniques are adopted. It is precisely the
seriousness of the historical discourse and the
quality of the evocations and reconstitutions that
determined this project's approach. Furniture
and textile historians, architects, archeologists,
and specialized companies were convened to
bring their knowledge and participate in making
the Women's Gallery a place for truly exploring a

historical interpretation of Chenonceau. The
aim was to provide visitors with the knowledge
necessary for fully discovering the estate, while
letting the monument, which preserves its
complete autonomy, speak for itself. In short, the
project deliberately inscribed itself into a harmonious dialectic between historical evocations
and contemporary set material.

The layout of the Women's Gallery unfolds like a
tour-walk with unpredictable evolutions, which
take into account the pleasure of wandering
about. Here, no particular route is imposed.
Instead, the visitor is encouraged to lose himself
and withdraw into the various parts of the set
design. Depending on one's desires, availability,
and needs, the visitor can dip into the information
he wants . . . even if the set design does insidiously
lure the visitor to bury himself in the documents
presented, longer than planned. The space is
organized by partitions that remain open, thus
exposing the arrangement of the original walls.
Without trying to enclose or direct the visitor, the
partitions allow the gaze to move between the
various stages of the visit, thus inducing a feeling
of freedom and fluidity that encourages and

continued on page 50

This engraving
of Jacques Androuet
du Cerceau's Grand
Project shows the colossal
extensions that Catherine
de Médicis began at
Chenonceau around
1576. The Women's
Gallery is located in the
outbuildings represented
above, which are
the only vestiges of this
ambitious program
of expansion.

Opposite page: Staged
in skits, illustrious
figures invite visitors to
discover the castle's
important historical
moments. Here,
Catherine de Médicis
entrusts Bernard Palissy
with the design of the
gardens and several
backdrops for festivities:
grottoes with cast
animals, fountains,
moving sculptures, etc.

Although they were thoroughly reworked during the nineteenth century, the outbuildings still possess the general spatial arrangement they had in the Renaissance. An awning of sixteenth-century inspiration has been added to reinforce the presence of this facade and complement its magnificent architectural ornamentation.

GALERIE DES DAMES
←

LA FERME DU XVIᵉ SIÈCLE
THE 16ᵀᴴ CENTURY FARM →

the monument: architects, painters, sculptors, decorators; and even the intellectuals and learned men who frequented the estate, whether they be writers, philosophers, or artists. Thus, along with the Women of Chenonceau, we find Francis I, Louis XIV, as well as Philibert de l'Orme, Primaticcio, Bernard Palissy, Rousseau, Voltaire, Flaubert . . .

The twelve scenes are pretexts for grouping together certain figures, but above all they open up wider historical perspectives on the society and art of the time: Francis I's visit reminds us of the king's control over the kingdom's big financiers; the tête-à-tête between Henry II and Diane de Poitiers sheds some light on the influencial role played by mistresses in the royal court; Diane de Poitiers in her *studiolo* stages the influence of Italian art during the early sixteenth century and in the construction of the royal palaces in the Loire valley; Primaticcio and Philibert de l'Orme in their studios illustrate Renaissance modes of production for art works; Catherine de Médicis and Bernard Palissy introduce the luxurious element of Renaissance parks and gardens; Catherine de Médicis's ball reveals how celebrations had an important role in governing; Louise of Lorraine in mourning introduces the religious dimension of the dawn of the seventeenth century; the huntsman Louis XIV pursues the Loire valley's hunting tradition . . .

Set Design

Numerous levels of readings accompany the discovery of these scenes, ranging from some dates and basic historical points of reference to pieces of information that go deep into the representation of history, for those who wish to do so. For example, within the setting of a reconstituted eighteenth-century salon, Rousseau and Voltaire's stays at Chenonceau evoke the intellectual society of the Enlightenment, the role of literary salons and their integration into French provincial life, the relationships that could develop between the world of finance and that of theater and philosophy, and aristocrats' patronage of intellectuals. By illustrating the presence of these two philosopher-writers at Chenonceau, these tableaux recall the literary soirées at the castle, Rousseau's role as the tutor of Madame Dupin's children, and his naturalist experiments.

The contrast between the soberness of the contemporary materials used in the set design (metal barriers, silk-screened glass for the sign-

fosters discovery. Frequently, windows in the partitions offer up new and privileged viewpoints that frame objects, fragments, and details.

Twelve Scenes

A tour of the Women's Gallery is divided into twelve scenes in which the women and famous historical figures who built and inhabited Chenonceau meet. These "moments" were chosen on the basis of a desire to represent the castle's owners: kings and queens of France, great aristocrats; the master craftsmen who built

Below: Every historical scene illustrates a specific moment in Chenonceau's history but they also give insight to the grand traditions of the royal courts as a whole. Here is one of the famous balls organized by Catherine de Médicis.

Opposite page: They also show the luxurious textiles and clothing of the time: velour, brocade, silk, passementerie, jewels, embroidery, etc.

age, plaster partitions, etc.) and the richness of materials deeply infused with historical evocations was deliberately developed out of a desire for elegance.

Historians and archeologists worked on the textiles and were able to reconstitute this ancient clothing with an almost unrivalled veracity. It necessitated several hundreds of fabrics from France and Italy, faithful copies of ancient models: silk velour, trimmed brocade and brocatelle, lampa and damask, antique satin, bleached and glazed linen . . . Specialized artisans were called upon to research and reconstitute the historical passementeries, the jewels decorating the clothes, the embroidery and lace.

Royal Court Life Re-Created

Accompanying the figures and setting off the richness of the fabrics, a few elements of décor and furniture contribute to creating a more realistic dimension. Diane de Poitiers deeply contemplates her antique bronzes in the setting of her *studiolo* made of precious wood inlay, Philibert de l'Orme is surrounded by his plans and etchings of the ancient monuments upon which he based his buildings' facades, Bernard Palissy studies the anatomic molds made from living animals that he was to use for creating the ornamentation of his magnificent Fountain of the Rock . . .

Creating a space for interpretation implies that one can discover a certain amount of "substance," which frequently translates into playing down the monument's interior decorations and details. Often empty, sometimes filled with some scattered pieces of furniture, or decorated by tapestries at best, monuments now rarely present the decorative whole that once constituted them. The density and arrangement of furniture is no long the same, the precise rules that organized the hierarchy between the elements of décor are not respected, many "expendable" objects have disappeared, such as curtains or wall hangings, color wash, or mats.

By means of the great care brought to the reproduction of décor, the Women's Gallery allows visitors to rediscover this density and see how the scenes of royal court life or private life were inscribed into a specific environment, today reconstituted as faithfully as possible to the reality of that time.   D. M.

The ceiling in Louise of Lorraine's bedchamber recalls the queen's mourning. It has all the traditional characteristics: wooden coffers painted with a gloomy dark color, burr motifs evoking Christ's crown of thorns, drops of blood, silver tears, etc.

Opposite page: In mourning the death of her husband, King Henry III, in 1589, Louise of Lorrraine transformed Chenonceau into a place of prayer and meditation. Nonetheless, the White Lady, who donned the color reserved for royal mourning, did not do away with luxury. Though austere in appearance, her clothes display meticulous craftsmanship: white and ivory silk threads, embroidery with pearls and passementeries, etc.

Nature Sets the Stage

The gardens of Chenonceau had their golden age in the sixteenth century.

Diane de Poitiers and Catherine de Médicis had them filled with rare plants and trees and

transformed them into settings for extravagant celebrations. By Ivan Cloulas.

The sparkle and the song of flowing water, the coolness of shade, and the rustling of foliage lend Chenonceau an indescribable charm. A subtle spell enchants visitors the moment they step onto the long majestic avenue of elms and plane trees leading to the castle's elegant facade.

Leaving behind the stately row of outbuildings to the right, they come upon the fifteenth-century donjon posted like a sentinel on its rock base just beyond the drawbridge. Rising out of the riverbed of the Cher, the fortified mill that oversaw the river's flow was converted into a castle by Thomas Bohier, controller general of finances for Normandy and administrator of revenues from the duchy of Milan under Francis I. His wife, Katherine Briçonnet, supervised the construction between 1513 and 1521, but neither she nor her son Antoine, who was forced to cede the castle to Francis I, had time to lay out the entries to the residence. The model for the latest fashion in floral decoration, however, was provided by the royal Châteaux of Ambroise and Blois, where Girolamo of Naples and Pacello de Mercagliano,

Begun in 1552, Diane de Poitiers's garden was planted on an elevated terrace that protects it from the rising waters of the Cher. Large quantities of earth were piled up to form a square, which is surrounded by a thick wall topped with a walkway.

the two gardeners whom Charles VIII brought from Italy, planted green gardens with paths, terraces, and arbors converging on fountains and bath-houses. Chenonceau could not ignore this trend: in the course of the sixteenth century, it was enhanced with three vast parks covering a total of eighty hectares.

When Diane de Poitiers received the castle in 1547, the estate contained no more than an acre of vegetable garden. This tiny, rustic space could

hardly accommodate courtly visits to Chenonceau. In order to provide her guests with a royal garden, the duchess selected what was then a barley field measuring two hectares, to the east of the castle. Located on the right bank of the Cher, it provided a magnificent view of the castle's east facade, while its proximity to the residence allowed for easy access. The site had one flaw, however: it was prone to flooding. Thus the first task, undertaken in the spring of 1551, consisted of protecting it from the river with a dirt levee reinforced with wooden piles. This forms one side of a vast square bordered on the other three sides by trenches that receive the waters of the Cher. The dirt piled up within the square then served as a base for the solidly dressed raised terraces.

The enormous project employed all the available workers in the area: carpenters, masons, carters, turfers, shovelers, stone-haulers, and laborers. In all, they were paid for more than fourteen thousand days of work, and the cost reached the considerable sum of 3,055 Tourainese livres. Eleven hundred loads of turf and seven thousand of stone rubble were transported by "rolling stretchers" or "trucks" drawn by cables and stretchers with two wheels, which worked like a wheelbarrow.

The garden's layout was quite simple: two paths intersecting diagonally created four large triangles that were subdivided into geometric compartments. At the intersection of the two paths, a stream of water gushes from a fountain. The garden owed its beauty to an excellent selection of plants.

To accentuate the view of the castle's west facade (opposite page), Catherine de Médicis created a garden below the forecourt and the Marques tower. In addition to a central basin (right and below), the queen integrated numerous curiosities among the square plots of flowers and shrubs: an aviary, a menagerie, a sheepfold, and Bernard Palissy's Fountain of the Rock.

Right: This building,
which dates from
the sixteenth century,
has served many
different functions.
Today it houses a flower
shop and storage space.

Below: One of the
buildings built for the
sixteenth-century farm,
with the vegetable
garden in the foreground.

In 1552, the archbishop of Tours and his vicar-general, Jean de Selve, a friend and patron of the renowned potter Bernard Palissy, brought gifts of plants and cuttings. Other powerful lords soon followed their example. Young sproutings were fertilized with seven bushels of oats to encourage the transplants. Thirteen thousand hawthorn and hazel shrubs were uprooted from the woods to form the hedges and arbors.

The archbishop's gardener decorated the beds with flowers and shrubs, including six peach-apricot trees, three hundred apple trees, eight loads of currant bushes, a hundred musk rose bushes, and another hundred lily bulbs. He added nine thousand wild strawberry and violet plants gathered from the woods. Two other gardeners working at the castle, Charlot Guérin and Jacques Dutertre, planted the square plot with a deluxe vegetable garden where artichokes and melons, which were then rare and reserved for princely tables, grew side by side with cucumbers, leeks, cabbage, peas, onions, shallots, and so forth. One hundred and fifty white mulberry trees were planted to feed silkworms for a future sericulture production. Thus utility was combined with pleasure.

The rabbit warren adjoining the flowerbed was transformed into a leisure park. At Diane's bidding, paths bordered with hawthorn and hazel trees were cut through it. Here and there, arbored nooks offered rest areas to strollers, who could lose themselves in the labyrinthine maze or amuse themselves with various games.

This beautiful ensemble, so carefully varied in its plan and floral composition, took five years to complete. The cost was more than five thousand livres, but the result was worthy of all praise.

King Henry II did not live to inaugurate this marvel.

Planted with hawthorn and hazel bushes, peach and apple trees, current bushes, wild strawberries, and violets, Diane's garden (above and left) also hosted five hundred white mulberry trees for the cultivation of silkworms.

Wounded in a tournament, he died in Paris on 10 July 1559, and Diane, to her great regret, had to return Chenonceau to her rival, the queen Catherine de Médicis.

When she took possession of the castle, Queen Catherine tried to overshadow the splendor of Diane's achievements with a grandiose celebration. On Sunday, 31 March 1560, she welcomed the young King Francis II and his wife, Mary Stuart, to her new estate. Triumphal arches, obelisks, columns, statues, and fountains were set up before the castle. As night fell, the youthful sovereigns, followed by the entire court, made their entrance under a shower of fireworks. With drums beating and banners unfurling in the black and white colors of the widowed queen, they were greeted by nine hundred servants and peasants grouped into well-ordered units. The main avenue was strewn with foliage, violets, and pinks. Flares, rockets, twisters, and girandoles lit up the branches of two huge oak trees flanked by obelisks. The royal procession crossed the bridge and entered the forecourt. A beacon in the form of an antique pillar lit the terrace. To the left, near the wooden bridge leading to Diane's garden, stood an altar decorated with branches of cypress, pine, pomegranate, and boxwood – Pluto's sacred trees meant to recall Catherine's bereavement. On the column above the altar, a gold Medusa's head coifed with entwined snakes made yet another allusion to the queen who courageously governed France in the midst of warring factions.

In front of the castle, statues of nymphs poured out light red wine. A young woman representing Fame stepped forward to congratulate the king. An Athena scattered bouquets of flowers to the wind. As this royal entry shows, Catherine de Médicis sought to use the gardens as the setting for a fantastic theater where celebrations and spectacles were to take place. In mid-April 1563, the entry of Charles IX revived this decorative

It took five years and five thousand livres to achieve Diane's garden (left and right), a varied ensemble of shaded rest areas in arbored nooks, labyrinthine mazes, and spaces for playing games.

program of using the gardens as a setting for balls, promenades by the water, fireworks, and masquerades. A third celebration, in May 1577, featured a transvestite banquet with King Henry III duly curled, pomaded, and dressed as a woman in shimmering fabrics.

When Catherine decided to incorporate the original castle into a complex of colonnades and wings, the distinguished architect Jean Bullant designed the plan that was later engraved by Jacques Androuet du Cerceau. Only one section was to be completed, however: the gallery that topped Diane's bridge over the Cher and the outbuildings. The castle's facade was decorated with four ancient divinities inviting visitors to cross the river and discover the queen's new project, the "garden of delight" created by Bernard Palissy.

While Catherine was away on a long voyage through France, her gardeners transformed the small valley of Francueil, which is located across from the castle, on the left bank. The formerly wild terrain was divided into uniform beds and the Vestin spring running through the center was joined by the waters of two lovely fountains. The lower slopes were lined with grottoes. At the top of

the hill was an amphitheater crowned with a high path. Evergreen bushes bordered the walkways. On the right bank, to the left of the castle entrance, was the Bohiers' former garden near the Marques tower. A thicket of pines, yew trees, boxwoods, and rosemary transformed it into a grove while holm oaks and olive trees were added to the more sheltered areas. In summer, they brought out the potted orange and lemon trees raised in a green-house the rest of the year. This was Catherine's "green garden," complete with an enormous aviary, a menagerie, and a sheepfold.

Behind the tower was the Fountain of the Rock, an artificial grotto decorated with stalactites and water creatures in enameled terra cotta – frogs, tortoises, crawfish, and serpents – similar to those found in the grottoes of Italian palaces. Inside, streams of water rising from the rock were col-lected in basins. To keep the fountain supplied, the queen installed underground pipes bringing in Dagrenière spring water, at great expense. For receptions, a vast table covered in enameled tiles was piled with food and flowers. Two projecting ledges, one on top of the other, formed terraces; the upper one was covered with vines and

enclosed with a wall decorated with columns, statues, and bench-lined niches.

From then on, the gardens enveloped Chenonceau with a setting of greenery, water, and flowers. But with the passage of time and the lack of upkeep, the parks and gardens fell into wilderness. For more than a century, Diane and Catherine's embellishments faded into a state of neglect.

The eighteenth century, however, brought with it a renewed enthusiasm for nature. Louise Dupin decided to make the estate an enormous dream park. There, Jean-Jacques Rousseau, her son's tutor, wrote a comedy and some poems, including one that extols the beauty of Sylvie's Path, which borders the Cher to the west of the castle:

As I wander in these groves, / How my heart feels exquisite pleasure! / How I enjoy myself in this leafy shade, / How I love these silvery streams! / Sweet and charming reverie, / Dear beloved solitude, / May you forever charm me![1]

Louise Dupin passed away at the castle on 20 November 1799; it was her wish to remain on

Above and left: Basins and detail of a basin in Diane's garden. The garden was never to be inaugurated by the king: wounded in a tournament, Henry II died in 1559 and his mistress was forced to hand over the estate to the widowed queen.

Opposite page: Now covered by plane trees instead of elms, the magnificent avenues, which once served as settings for Catherine de Médicis's extravagant celebrations, are still lined by canals.

Right: At the east end of Diane's garden, a drawbridge crosses a moat flowing into the Cher.

Left: Athena, Apollo, Hercules, and Cybele, the caryatids that Catherine de Médicis had placed in the middle of the castle's facade. Three centuries later, Marguerite Pelouze decided to relegate them to the edge of the park.

Next double page: Aerial view of the entire estate. We can distinguish between Diane's garden, which is east of the castle, and that of Catherine de Médicis, west of the castle.

the estate and be buried in a romantic tomb in the park on the bank of the Cher river .

The time of rebirth for the Renaissance gardens was finally to come with Marguerite Pelouze, who restored the castle and the flowerbeds to their former state of glory. By the time the thirteen-year restoration was completed in 1878, the castle had lost the caryatids installed by Catherine de Médicis – Hercules, Athena, Apollo, and Cybele found their place in the park. Strangely detached from their architecture and aligned with the backside of a tree-covered

walkway, they remind the visitor of the splendor of the royal entries, at a time when these same gods, incarnated as handsome mortals, descended from Olympus to take up residence, for the space of one celebration, in the gardens of Chenonceau.   I. C.

1. Qu'à m'égarer dans ces bocages / Mon cœur goûte de voluptés! / Que je me plais sous ces ombrages / Que j'aime ces flots argentés! / Douce et charmante rêverie / Solitude aimable et chérie / Puissiez-vous toujours me charmer!

A Historical Visit

A tour of Chenonceau starts off in a large vestibule. To the right is the Louis XIV salon, which notably houses Ruben's *Jesus and St. John,* and the bedchamber of Francis I, where we can admire *The Three Graces* by Van Loo and *Diane de Poitiers* by Primaticcio. To the left, there is Diane de Poitiers's bedchamber, which leads to Catherine de Médicis's Green Study and library and a Guardroom decorated with seventeenth-century Flemish tapestries. The latter, which was renovated during the eighteenth century, opens onto a small chapel with a triangular apse.

In the extension of the ground floor, we come to Catherine de Médicis's eighteen-window bridge-gallery. At its southern extremity, a false mantelpiece surrounds a door that opens onto the left bank of the Cher. The kitchens, which were installed in the hollow piers, adjoin a platform built at water level to allow for direct delivery of merchandise brought by boat.

A Renaissance staircase of Italian inspiration leads to the second floor. Like the ground floor, it begins with a vestibule decorated with eighteenth-century tapestries from Audenarde and opens onto four rooms: to the right, the bedchambers of César de Vendôme and Gabrielle d'Estrées and, to the left, we have Catherine de Médicis's bedchamber, which adjoins a print room containing engravings of Chenonceau, and the Bedchamber of the Five Queens, nicknamed as such in memory of the queen mother's two daughters and three daughters-in-law. As for the third floor, it contains only one room: Louise of Lorraine's bedroom. This reconstitution was based on the remains of a ceiling whose white on black emblems of sorrow bear witness to how she mourned her husband's death to her dying day.

Right: The capitals in the central gallery are richly adorned with motifs of Italian inspiration.

Below: The Louis XIV salon. This room was thus named in honor of the Sun King's visit to Chenonceau on 14 July 1650. On the Renaissance fireplace, the Salamander and Ermine evoke the memory of Francis I and his queen, Claude de France.

Installed in the enormous
hollow piers of Thomas
Bohier's square loggia,
the Renaissance kitchens
(above) were furnished
with modern equipment
during the First World
War, when the castle was
converted into a hospital.
The biggest fireplace in
the whole castle is to be
found in the butlery (left).

Above: The Women's Gallery, recently installed in the Dome buildings. In her studiolo, Diane de Poitiers sets the stage for a strong Italian influence in early-sixteenth-century art. In the background, Philibert de l'Orme works in his studio.

Left: The wine storehouse. Today, Chenonceau's vineyards cover more than thirty hectares. The wine produced by the castle is designated *Appellation d'origine contrôlée Touraine.*

The drawbridge that leads to the valley of Francueil, where Catherine de Médicis built an ampitheater on its summit.

Right: The bridge built by Diane de Poitiers between 1555 and 1559 joins the castle to the gardens planted on the uneven slopes of the Cher's left bank.

Back cover: Vestiges of the floor tiling laid in the Guardroom in the nineteenth century.

General Information

Château de Chenonceau, 37150 Chenonceaux. Tel: 02 47 23 90 07. Fax: 02 47 23 80 88. Website: www.chenonceau.com.
The castle is located on the Cher river, 214 kilometers from Paris and 34 kilometers from Tours.
How to get to Chenonceau:
By car. Take freeway A 10 (the Aquitaine freeway), exit at Blois or Amboise, 2 hours from Paris or 30 minutes from Tours.
By TGV (high-speed train) Paris-Montparnasse–Saint-Pierre-des-Corps, 1 hour. By TER (regular train) Tours–Chenonceaux, 25 minutes.
The castle is open all year round:
February 1–15, 9:00 AM–5:00 PM. February 16–28, 9:00 AM–5:30 PM. March 1–15, 9:00 AM–6:00 PM. March 16–September 15, 9:00 AM–7:00 PM. September 16–30, 9:00 AM–6:30 PM. October 1–15, 9: 00 AM–6:00 PM. October 16–31, 9:00 AM–5:30 PM. November 1–15, 9:00 AM–5:00 PM. November 16–January 31, 9:00 AM–4:30 PM.
Activities: The sound and light show *In the Time of the Ladies of Cheonceau* is presented every night (July 1–August 31). During summer, there are also boat rides on the Cher. The cellar is open from March 16 to early November.

For further reading: ·

Annie Cosperec, *Les châteaux de la Loire,* Editions Hermé, 1997, 203 pages.
Jean-Baptiste Leroux, Pierre Miquel, *Les châteaux de la Loire panoramiques,* Editions du Chêne, 1999, 176 pages.
Colette Gauvion, *Châteaux en Val de Loire,* Editions du Chênes, 1986, 160 pages.
Ivan Cloulas, *Les châteaux de la Loire au temps de la Renaissance,* Editions Hachette Littératures, 1999, 354 pages.
Michel Mélot, *Châteaux en Pays de Loire,* Editions Evergreen, 1997, 208 pages.
Milena Ercole Pazzoli, *Les châteaux de la Loire,* Editions Gründ, 1996, 144 pages.
L'ABCdaire des châteaux de la Loire, Editions Flammarion, 1996, 120 pages.
Noël Graveline, *Le grand livre des châteaux de la Loire,* Editions Minerva, 1993, 192 pages.
S. Chiral, P. Seydoux, *Le Val de Loire des châteaux et des manoirs,* Editions du Chêne, 1991, 232 pages.

CONNAISSANCE DES ARTS – Numéro hors série (H. S. 37). RÉDACTEUR EN CHEF: Philip JODIDIO. RESPONSABLE HORS SÉRIE: Sylvie BLIN. SECRÉTAIRE GÉNÉRALE DE LA RÉDACTION: Danielle MARTI. SECRÉTAIRE DE RÉDACTION: Caroline BRAUD. DIRECTRICE ARTISTIQUE: Sandrine RONDARD. MAQUETTE: Marie-Laure RESNAIS. SERVICE PHOTOS: Martine JOSSE. SECRÉTARIAT: Inès DUVAL, Kathryn LEVESQUE. DIRECTEUR TECHNIQUE: Christian LECOCQ. DIRECTEUR COMMERCIAL: Philippe THOMAS. TRADUCTION: Elizabeth Jian-Xing TOO et Miriam ROSEN.

ONT COLLABORÉ À CE NUMERO: Ivan CLOULAS, Alain DECAUX, Axelle de GAIGNERON, Jean GUILLAUME, Didier MOULIN, Bernard VOISIN.

CRÉDITS PHOTOS. COUVERTURE et pages 2, 4, 5, 6-7, 8, 9, 10, 12-3, 14-5, 16, 21, 22-3, 25, 27, 28-9, 33, 34, 35, 36,37bs,38, 39, 40, 41, 42-3, 48-9,51, 52, 53, 56, 58, 59, 60, 63, 67,70dr, 71bs, 72, 73, 74, 75, 76: Arnaud Carpentier. P. 3, 11, 12,18-9, 20, 30, 31, 32, 37ht, 44-5, 62 , 64, 65, 66, 71ht: Jacqueline Guillot. P.17, 23, 24: Bibliothèque Nationale de France. P. 26, 54-5, 57, 61, 70g: Photoflash Pro. P.46, 50 : Bernard Saint-Genès. P. 47: DR P.68-9: R.Van Der Meeren/Altitude .

© 2001 Société Française de Promotion Artistique, 23, rue des Jeûneurs, 75002 Paris. Tél.: 01 44 88 55 00. Fax: 01 44 88 51 88. e-mail: cda@cdesarts.com. R. C. Paris 75 B 4306 Seine. Direction de la publication: C. Lecocq. Commission paritaire: 1005 K 79964 ISSN 1242-9198. Dépôt légal: 2ᵉ trim. 2001. Imprimé en France par. Etic, à Laval (53). Photogravure: Boréal Graphic, Bourg-la-Reine.